Books in the

Let's Ask Auntie Anne Series

Let's Ask Auntie Anne

How to Raise a Moral Child

Book Five

Gary and Anne Marie Ezzo
with Diane Wiggins

Let's Ask Auntie Anne
How to Raise A Moral Child

Published by Parent-Wise Solutions, Inc. *(Parent-Wise Solutions*
is a division of the Charleston Publishing Group, Inc.)

International Standard Book Number:

1-932740-02-3

Printed in the United States of America

For information:
Parent-Wise Solutions, Inc.
2130 Cheswick Lane, Mt. Pleasant, SC 29466

04 05 06 07—7 6 5 4 3 2 1

Dedicated to…

David and Nancy Good
Forever our friends,
wise and true

Acknowledgements

Books are often a collaborative effort of many individuals whose gifts and talents help move a manuscript from scribbles to completion. This little book and the entire *Auntie Anne* series is no exception. We are indebted to a host of friends. First, we wish to thank Craig, Carly, Morgan, and Evan Wiggins for allowing wife and Mom time to work on the Auntie Anne series. Their sacrifice gave Diane the opportunity to use her creative giftedness. We also offer a hearty thank you to our wonderful editors Judith St. Pierre and Jennifer Gott. Joining them in proof reading is our dear friend Suzanne Johns and family and Michelle Warner. And last but not least, the one who inspired the completion of the series is our beloved Auntie Anne. May her Scrabble board never grow cold.

Series Prologue

Author's Notes

Meet the Real Auntie Anne

Meet the Carriage Couples

Author's Notes

⁂

In this series of books we depart from our traditional method of dialectic instruction, (premise, facts, argument and conclusion) and turn to an older and more personal style of persuasion—sharing parenting principles in story-form. Who doesn't love a good story?

Stories are entertaining and provide a unique conduit for dispensing practical wisdom and moral truth that otherwise might be lost in an academic venue. When we read or hear a story we find ourselves feeling for the characters through their speech and thoughts. We often identify and empathize with their fears, hopes, dreams and expectations. Most importantly, from their successes and failures we can learn lessons for life. Stories have the power to change us—and indeed they do!

The *Let's Ask Auntie Anne* series consist of five stories and five pertinent parenting themes. Each story is embedded with practical advice that will guide the reader to greater understanding of the complexities of childrearing and hopefully serve as a friend to motivate positive change.

Finally, the series was designed for individual or group study. The questions at the end of each book both remind and highlight the significant principles of the lessons taught. Whether you read for your own pleasure or share with a community of friends, we know you will benefit from a trip to Auntie Anne's kitchen and her treasury of parenting knowledge. Enjoy.

Gary and Anne Marie Ezzo
Mt. Pleasant, South Carolina
August 2004

Meet the Real Auntie Anne

⁓

Eleanor Roosevelt insightfully concluded that "Beautiful young people are accidents of nature, but beautiful old people are works of art." The main character in this book is, as the former First Lady described, a beautiful work of art, fashioned by the colors of life.

Auntie Anne is not a fictional character. She was born in Boston, Massachusetts, on March 24, 1914. Her life, while not as glamorous as Eleanor Roosevelt's has indeed been greatly influential. With an earthly common sense that often eludes others and a sense of humor that never fails, this amazing woman of ninety-plus years continues to endear herself to friend and stranger.

Each book in this series is as much a tribute to a beautiful life as it is a parenting resource filled with timeless wisdom and practical application. In each story (just as in real life), Auntie Anne is cheerfully spry, physically capable, neither failing in sight nor mind. A philosopher of sorts, and like those of her day, her interest extends into all areas. The mind, she believes, has no limits but those we choose to give it, and hungry minds, whether of children or the elderly, need the food of useful knowledge—*daily*.

In real life, the children who called Auntie Anne "Mom" were children of aristocrats, professors, and other notables from the fair cities up North. No, they were not her children by birth, but by design. As a Boston nanny, she loved them as a mother loves her own. She would weave buttercup crowns and sing treasured melodies. She cooked extravagantly and lusciously—spices and herbs, warm buttered bread, and crusty apple cobbler baked to a beautiful brown hue. Reading followed mealtimes routinely. Each of the children under Auntie Anne's care were taught to love books. She took them through literary adventures with Dickens, Poe, T. S. Eliot, Tolkien, Hemingway, Bunyan, and more.

The beautiful, historical City of Charleston, South Carolina, frames the backdrop for the series. Auntie Anne draws her parenting lessons from the city's rich history and the daily life of people living on or near the Carolina saltwater marshes. Charleston's glorious past from the Colonial period through the American Revolution, the Civil War, and into the present day and the beauty of its perfectly maintained historical district, cobblestone streets and waterfront parks are all woven into Auntie Anne's lessons.

From her kitchen window she overlooks the wide green marsh and the blue waters of the Wando River in the lovely neighboring town of Mt. Pleasant. The descriptions of places, scenes, and the anecdotal stories in each book are factual. Apart from Auntie Anne, the characters in our stories are fictional but their needs accurately reflect the many common concerns and challenges for today's parents. The authors speak through Auntie Anne's life story to satisfy the needs of each inquiring couple.

Come and enjoy. Put on your slippers, find a quiet nook, and benefit from a trip to RiverTowne, and Auntie Anne's kitchen. If you can picture a home by the water, a flowered paradise of sorts, with a vista of blue skies and green marshes, where birds and butterflies fill the air and the scent of ocean mingles with a Carolina morning, then you have successfully imagined Auntie Anne's home at the water's edge. Here you will find a friend, one who connects for a new generation of parents the *descriptive*—the way it was and the way it is—with the *prescriptive*—the way it should be.

Meet the Carriage Couples

I t all goes back to Missy. Of course, she could not have known the train of events to spin out of her spunky fondness for hopping in cars not her own. Nor does she own a car. This Missy, oh beg your pardon, is a dog. A fluffy white pedigree peek-a-poo with a Rottweiler complex and a James Cagney smile.

When she hopped in the car of Geoff and Ginger Portier on that Saturday night so long ago, no one could have imagined the chain of events that would eventually lead five couples on a journey of discovery about themselves and their parenting. In one of life's paradoxical moments, the beginning often becomes clearer in light of the end and so it is with our story.

It was through the strange encounter with Missy, that the Portiers first met Auntie Anne. (Narrative is found in Book Five.) It only took one delightful Sunday afternoon sipping sweet tea and playing a game of Scrabble for Geoff and Ginger to discover the treasury of Auntie Anne's knowledge.

Auntie Anne is more than a good person at heart and

a wonderful chef in the kitchen, she is also a wise sage, a woman gifted in thought with a plentiful supply of grace and charm. All of this accented by a marvelous wit. Yes, a refreshing wit that compliments her clean heart and noble mind.

In a time of desperation and perplexing challenges our dear Auntie Anne brings much needed correction and aid to Geoff and Ginger's parenting. From that experience, others would come to know of this woman's marvelous gifts.

The following Spring five couples crowded together on the padded seats of an old wooden carriage harnessed to two brown mules named Knick and Knack. Two-week-old chicks circled underfoot, pecking eagerly at feed dropped from the mules' grain bags.

A minute later, the driver shook the reins and called, "Eeyuup." Twenty-two-hundred pounds of muscle lunged forward as chicks scattered in every direction. The carriage swayed out of the big red barn to the rhythm of creaking wood and clopping hoofs. Another tour of historical Charleston, South Carolina had begun with a promise of a blessing.

Coincidence or destiny? It mattered little. It was just one of those odd occurrences in life. Five couples, strangers to each other, meet randomly on a bright and sunny Carolina morning and everything clicked. A few minutes into the carriage ride and the couples were already talking about their children left at home. School pictures traveled up and down the rows greeted by smiles and nodding heads. The tour of Charleston's historical district took just over an hour and by the time the carriage returned to the big red barn, the couples were talking like old friends. Charleston has a way of doing that, making everyone feel like family.

It was Geoff and Ginger Portier who brought up the idea of lunch. Eyes met and heads nodded and before long, five couples set out to enjoy one of the Charleston's delightful bistros. Settling in with iced chai, and a few diet cokes, the couples talked about the high points of the tour before the topic turned once again to their children, parenting and life on the home-front.

It was than that Geoff and Ginger directed the conversation by sharing what they considered to be one of Charleston's best kept secrets.

"Her name," Geoff said, "is Auntie Anne and she can change your life. Her thoughts are relevant, her searching mind insightful, and her understanding of the human heart runs deep and wide."

"She is a refreshing change from all the parenting experts I've read lately," Ginger added, "and her wise counsel is gentle and affective."

"If you need help with parenting, and find yourself frustrated with your other options, pay a little visit to Auntie Anne. There are only two things required," Geoff went on to say. "First, play a game of Scrabble with the dear woman and second, talk nice to her little dog Missy."

Geoff and Ginger continued with their celebration of Auntie Anne, sharing about that memorable Sunday afternoon months ago. The contagious energy of their enthusiasm was food for the weary soul and put hope and expectancy in the hearts of their new friends. Now peeked with curiosity and a secret longing for assistance, each couple over time would find their way to the big green house near the water's edge. The place where Auntie Anne calls home.

There are five couples and five unique parenting challenges. Listen in as Auntie Anne satisfies each inquiry with relevant and practical "rubber meets the road" advice.

In Book One, Mac and Vicki Lake can not figure out why their children act as if they are not loved. Mom and Dad are missing something so basic that even the simple phrase "I love you" falls short of its intended meaning. How well did Auntie Anne help them? You decide after reading *How to Raise a Loving Child.*

In Book Two, meet Bill and Elaine Lewis. Who doesn't know at least one family facing the frustration of irresponsible children? Messy rooms, wet towels on the floor, and unfinished homework are just the beginning. Join Bill and Elaine as they go with Auntie Anne on a journey to the heart of *How to Raise a Responsible Child.*

In Book Three, little do Rick and Lela Harvey know that a lack of security is the root of their children's behavioral problems. Nervous, irritable children acting out at school in seemingly uncontrollable ways are a dead giveaway. Auntie Anne has a plan for this home. Find out what and *who* needs to change in *How to Raise a Secure Child.*

In Book Four, Clarke and Mia Forden seek out Auntie Anne's advice on building trusting relationships. For Clarke and Mia, the pace of today's family is troubling. How will fathers capture the hearts of their children with so little time? Find out what they wished they had learned a dozen years earlier in *How to Raise a Trusting Child.*

In Book Five, Geoff and Ginger Portier tell their story of how Auntie Anne taught them how to make virtues and values real in the lives of their children. What will it take to create a love for moral beauty within the heart of their children? Auntie Anne provides solid answers in *How to Raise a Moral Child.*

Introduction

If there was ever couple that expected to turn out top-notch kids, it's the Portiers. Geoff and Ginger have followed all the traditional avenues for success. They've read how-to books, attended seminars and sought the advice of experts on parenting. But somehow all their efforts haven't translated into what they most want to see in their children—strong moral values. Apparently they've missed something along the way, for their children show alarming signs that they lack a moral compass.

At twelve, Lizzie spends most of her time in front of the mirror, imagining how great she'd look if her parents would just allow her to dress like Britney Spears. She's cute and fun to be around, but her life has one central theme—Lizzie—and her folks worry about her inability to see beyond herself. Son Carter, nearly eight, is a piece of work. Once upon a time this creative genius had amused everyone with the tales he made up. Little did Geoff and Ginger suspect that their son's fertile imagination would lead to a pattern of deception. Lies lurk in everything Carter says and no punishment seems enough to root them out.

Reality struck one day when Geoff and Ginger discovered that their parenting cruise control was set for crash and burn. A huge moral infraction, the kind that draws unwanted public attention, caused them to cross the line from concern to alarm. This just wasn't going to go away. Clearly, they had not succeeded in impressing upon their offspring moral standards that were acceptable to them—or to their neighbors.

That was the sad state of affairs in the Portier household the Saturday night a fluffy white adorable pedigree peek-a-poo puppy hopped into their car and changed their lives forever.

~ The Reunion ~

RB's on Shem Creek was the perfect venue for the carriage couples reunion. Their table afforded a panoramic view of the Mount Peasant waterway and beyond. Shrimp boats were moored for the night, their shining nets folded like bat wings caught the attention of an occasional gull. A sail boat slowly worked its way up the creek, past a row of restaurants spilling out sounds of chatter and the scent of good food. Just outside the window, a lone pelican roosted on a green piling, unaffected by the coming and going of visitors.

No one really paid much attention to the outside splendor—not now—not with Ginger's eyes misting with unbidden tears and Geoff listening intently. The carriage couples were paying tribute to their benefactors.

"Words can not express how much the two of you mean to us Geoff. If it wasn't for you and Ginger, well, we don't know where our families would be today." Clarke paused as seven heads nodded with all sincerity incapable of being counterfeited. "I know for Mia and myself, our visit with Auntie Anne changed our family forever. We went that day a little skeptical but we left humbled by her grace and charm."

"I think all of us at this table have on occasion played the 'what if?' game," Bill picked up were Clarke left off. "What if we never took that carriage ride ten months ago? What if we never met you? What if you never mentioned our dear Auntie Anne to us? What if we never met her? Where would we be today? We all knew we needed help in our parenting but none of us knew how much we needed Auntie Anne's wisdom. And the two of you are responsible for helping us discover that."

Lela placed a confetti-covered gift bag on the table. "Geoff and Ginger, this is from all us to you with love and hugs."

Reaching through the bright yellow tissue paper, Ginger removed a picture with a wooden frame, trimmed with etchings of the buildings along Rainbow Row.

Behind the glass were five smiling couples standing in front of a mule-drawn carriage with their arms around each other's shoulders. It was the carriage couples' first meeting.

"Oh Lela, this is beautiful," Ginger said, her eyes misting. "It was one of those moments of a lifetime, and now it's captured forever. Thank you, all of you."

Geoff took Ginger's hand and glanced appreciatively around the table. They both took in the moment with the full significance of the evening's celebration.

"I read somewhere that after every great victory, the ancient Israelites would build a monument out of a single stone and called it an Ebenezer stone that served as a reminder of their deliverance and God's goodness. Friends like you are the Ebenezer stones of our life, reminders of how fortunate we are to be together. My only regret of this evening is that Auntie Anne could not join us. She is the real reason why we are all together. After all, she is the one who pointed us in the right direction. I know for our family, it was no secret in the neighborhood about what things we needed to fix with our children. They lacked... how did you describe it Ginger?"

Ginger looked over and smiled. "They lacked moral sensibility."

"Yea, that's a nice way to say it Hon. It makes me

feel less guilty!" The couples laughed.

"Our kids knew all the right things to do but lacked the understanding of why they should do it. So, if it wasn't for Auntie Anne, well, none of us would be here tonight. She got this whole thing started."

Ginger took Geoff's hand and mouthed a thank you to the table of friends.

"You know Geoff," Clarke interrupted, "I never heard how you and Ginger came to meet Auntie Anne in the first place. So, you're saying it had something to do with moral training?"

"I've never heard the story either," Rick interrupted. "Maybe its time that we all hear how destiny brought the two of you to Auntie Anne's kitchen and scrabble board." All heads nodded in unison including Ginger's.

"Go ahead Hon. I still get goose pumps thinking about how it all happened and the first time we met Auntie Anne."

"Well, back up a little Ginger. It all began with the dog. Do you remember that night?"

"Oh, that was so strange," Ginger turned her head back to the four couples. "We were just dropping off some dessert for a community meeting being held next door to Auntie Anne's…."

"Is that Barbara's house?" Vicki blurted as if they

were old friends. "Remember Mac? We met Barbara on that morning. Her grandchildren were chasing leaping frogs over something."

"A tree frog Vicki, not a leaping frog," Mac corrected. "Now my sweet precious, let Ginger finish her story."

Vicki put two fingers to her lips. "Oops, sorry about that."

"Well, Geoff and I were only dropping the dessert off because we couldn't stay for the meeting. Remember what happened Geoff?"

"Do I ever. I stayed behind the wheel while Ginger took the dessert to Barbara. She left her door open. While she was on the porch, an adorable little white puppy, with big chocolate eyes came over to her side of the car. The next thing I know, she was sitting in Ginger's seat like a passenger ready to go for a ride."

"Missy!" Mia looked at Elaine. The carriage couples all had fond memories of Missy's antics in the kitchen. Elaine grinned when she remembered how Missy had picked up Mick the monkey by the tail and dragged him over to Auntie Anne so she could make a point about teaching children responsibility. Mia chuckled at the memory of Missy bringing Auntie Anne a gift of a magnolia bud. All she could see were the muddy paw prints on the kitchen floor, but all Auntie Anne saw was the joy in that puppy's eyes.

"It was Missy all right, "Ginger said. "When I got back to the car, she was sitting in my seat and looking up at me as if to ask, 'Where are we going?' Geoff took her to Barbara's to see if anyone knew whose dog she was. Barb recognized her immediately and pointed us to Auntie Anne's house."

Geoff picked up the story. "Well, to make a long story even longer, the gardeners had left the back gate open, and Missy, being the party dog she is, had found her way over to Barb's and then into our car. We met Auntie Anne when we took Missy home. The next day we received a plate of freshly baked biscotti's from Auntie Anne and a note thanking us for taking care of Missy,"

"Auntie Anne also invited us over for afternoon tea," Ginger added. "I called her, and while we were chit-chatting, I found out she played Scrabble. Geoff loves Scrabble but no one will play with him. So he was up for a visit. The kids were at my sister's place on Sullivan's Island for the day, so the afternoon was ours."

"We were just expecting to have some tea and play a game of Scrabble," Geoff said. "It was a lovely afternoon. I remember it well. We had no idea how that visit would change our lives."

~ The Sunday Visit ~

The beige golf cart puttered past the village green and along Victoria Row, so named for its display of elegant homes with sweeping verandas, colorful hanging flowers, and white picket fences. Here and there neighbors sat in comfortable Southern rockers, chatting and waving to passers-by. Geoff turned the cart down a side street and headed toward the big green house with black hurricane shutters.

Auntie Anne's yard was an exposition of color. The white picket fence was draped with Martha Vineyard roses that accented both sides of the roadside entrance with touches of bright pink blossoms. The hedges of Ligustrum lining the drive directed the visitors' eyes toward the piazza. Mandeville vines, with their tender blooms of white and red, wove their magic through the climbing spindles. Blue periwinkles in hanging baskets and four, inviting white rocking chairs completed the welcoming scene.

Geoff and Ginger followed the brick pathway to the front stoop and climbed the ten wide steps to the piazza. To the side of the door they noticed a small brass figure of an old monk standing at a church entrance. His folded hands grasped a small chain that when pulled rang a small bell. Neither Geoff nor Ginger took any time to ponder the meaning of this symbol, if that's what it was. Geoff knocked on the door.

Inside, the frisky eager greeting of a small dog was heard. "M i s s y," Ginger mouthed to Geoff who held her hand. Saying the creature's name felt familiar.

After a few moments, the barking stopped and a furry face appeared at a window, left of the door. Missy put her two front paws on the glass and stared out, tail wagging. In a moment, the big black door swung open and there she was, Auntie Anne. A warm smile greeted the two visitors.

"Well now, it's Mr. Geoff and Miss Ginger. Come in, come in," Auntie Anne said, as if welcoming long-lost friends. "How are the two of you doing on this lovely day?"

"We're doing just fine, thank you," Ginger replied in her sweet southern way. "It's so nice of you to have us over."

"Auntie Anne, are you sure you're up for this Scrabble match?" Geoff started. "I play a lot and I'm not an easy push over." Geoff rambled on while Ginger's eyes were directed to a variety of paintings prominently displayed near the entry way. When Geoff finally paused, Ginger inquired with a pointing finger, "Auntie Anne, did you paint all of these?"

"Oh no, not all of them. My art instructor back in Boston painted these two." Auntie Anne pointed to two of the paintings. "She was very talented. These three over here are my mistakes."

"Well, these are hardly mistakes." Ginger examined the rich detail of color and design. "They're beautiful."

A sweet trio of yaps confirmed the words and Ginger glanced down to see Missy straining her neck to observe the art in question. Almost subconsciously she took a step aside to allow the furry white creature an ample view.

Auntie Anne moved closer to Ginger and looked at her own work. "Oh my." Auntie Anne sounded almost startled.

"Is something wrong?" Ginger inquired with a touch of concern.

"No, no. I just saw the date on this one. I painted it before you and Geoff were even born. It's hard to believe that such a young person is living in this old body."

Having grasped the significance of what he had just heard, Geoff quickly did the math computing the years. "As far as I can see Auntie Anne, time only makes things around here more beautiful."

Auntie Anne slowly turned and offered an appreciative smile. "You know Mr. Geoff, if you keep saying sweet things like that I'm going to feel real bad about beating you at Scrabble."

Ginger smiled at Auntie Anne.

A series of loud beeps from the oven summoned her to the kitchen. "Oh please, make yourself at home. I have something in the oven to tend to."

Ginger stepped into the great room. Geoff followed, hands behind his back. The room was large and inviting, filled with shelves of mementos and heirlooms. A variety of philodendrons were placed everywhere, arranged to accent each nook, shelf, and table. One wall was covered in decorative frames displaying photographs of a younger woman long ago.

Drawn by the welcoming sound of a whistling tea kettle, Geoff and Ginger poked their heads into the kitchen. Around the corner, under the west-facing windows, was a table set for a tea party. Oversized porcelain teacups rested on hand-painted saucers depicting miniature roses and variegated ivy. In the center of the table stood a large rose-colored pitcher erupting with pink hydrangea. Auntie Anne bade her guests enter the enchanted room.

While Geoff and Ginger seated themselves, Auntie Anne set a woven sweetgrass basket on the table. Peeking out from the pink linen napkin lining the basket were golden brown banana-nut muffins, their crusted surfaces exploding with walnuts. "They're fresh from the oven. Please enjoy."

"Mmmm, this look so good," Ginger said. She took a muffin out of the basket, set it on her plate, and then looked down to smooth her pink and white checkered linen napkin across her lap.

Geoff suddenly looked out the window. "Look Ginger" Geoff prompted by pointing out over the water. As Ginger responded, searching the horizon for the cause of his outburst, Geoff reached before her, to slide away her muffin delight and place it next to his own.

Auntie Anne kept a straight face as she poured the boiling water into the porcelain teapot.

"I don't see anything," Ginger said turning to search Geoff's face. "What was it? A crane?"

"Oh, never mind," Geoff smiled tenderly patting her shoulder with the criminal hand. "It's gone now," he added, looking up to meet Auntie Anne's accusatory smirk.

"Hey wait a minute, Mr. Sneaky," Ginger said. "You stole my muffin!" She retrieved her plate, protecting it from Geoff with encircled hands.

Geoff laughed. "Sorry honey. One look at those muffins and I gave into temptation in a moment of hunger." Ginger reached over snapping Geoff's arm with her finger.

Auntie Anne set the teapot on the table and sat down. "Maybe it's a good thing you weren't the one who found that businessman's moneybag last week," she said.

"You must mean that story about young Heather Knowlton in the *Post and Carrier,*" Ginger said, impressed that Auntie Anne kept up on local current events. "The paper said her dad had been out of work for almost three months, so I'll bet her family had some pretty big needs. But every cent was returned to the police station."

"It sounded like a fairy tale to me," Geoff said, looking at Auntie Anne. "Did you read the quote from her dad? He said that the situation had tested Heather's heart and proved that it was in fine working order."

"Obviously, Heather's Dad and Mom instilled in her the moral courage to do the right thing." Auntie Anne pointed out as she poured steaming tea into each cup.

"Moral courage?" Geoff mused out loud. "Interesting use of words."

"Very definitely moral courage," Auntie Anne replied. "Moral courage planted deep in that young girl's heart led her to return all the money."

"If I had been out of work that long, I might have

hoped my kid would have offered ol' pop a few bills first," Geoff said. "You know, the 'charity starts at home' thing."

"But you wouldn't have accepted the money," Ginger said, "because it didn't belong to you. Right dear?"

"Yes, of course." Geoff smiled and gave his wife a reassuring pat on the back. "But I can't help wondering what our children would have done under the same circumstances Heather found herself in; finding a large amount of cash, no name or bank account number; who would have ever known?"

"Well Geoff, children do surprise us sometimes when they're tested," Auntie Anne said.

"If it takes the moral courage you talk about, I wouldn't want to test them. Not right now at least." Clarke turned to Ginger, "I think that's what might be missing with our kids "G'. You know what I mean?"

Ginger shook her head. "I'm not sure I do." She helped herself to the sugar and then slowly stirred her tea hoping someone would change the subject. Geoff's tendency to be transparent was showing itself again much to Ginger's chagrin. While her own two children demonstrated some moral control, she knew there was no way they could match Heather Knowlton's moral achievements.

"Well, if you ask this ninety year old woman, our

society as a whole is missing the richness of moral courage. People expect others, like Heather, to do the right thing, but they do not feel nor see the need to reciprocate."

Geoff nodded. "Moral courage. To be honest with you Auntie Anne, this is an area we're struggling in. I know something is missing with our kids, but I just can't put my finger on it."

Cringing at Geoff's candor, Ginger glanced over at him and raised her eyebrows. After all, this visit wasn't suppose to be about airing the family's dirty laundry. They were here for tea and Scrabble. That, she was comfortable with.

Noticing Ginger's demeanor, Auntie Anne turned to Geoff and asked, "You mean the same sticky finger that stole your wife's treat?"

Ginger laughed and began to relax. "Seriously, Auntie Anne," she said, "we try to be diligent when teaching our children right from wrong. But we're falling short. I sense it to."

"Yah, but Hon, let's not be too hard on ourselves. It's not just our children. Kids today in general act on impulse. Moral courage isn't happening anywhere, at least from what I can see."

"I think that children today are just like they have

always been," Auntie Anne said. "They are a reflection of the rest of us."

Geoff paused for a moment. "You mean, like the society as a whole?" he asked.

Auntie Anne slowly nodded. "That's part of it," she said. "As a whole, our society lacks moral courage. But there's even more to it than that." She set down her teacup and looked across the table. "Children's morals are a reflection of what's in Mom and Dad's heart."

"You mean it's about *us*?" Geoff asked, pointing to himself and Ginger.

"I'm afraid so," Auntie Anne said.

Geoff twitched. "Oh, Auntie Anne, that's kind of scary. But to tell you the truth, deep down inside, I've always felt that their moral choices are tied back to us in some way."

"From the beginning of time, moral education has always begun with Mom and Dad," Auntie Anne said before pausing a moment to take a sip of tea. "And don't be fooled by that new psychology that says it is not so. Moral training starts when parents decide which values are important to them and which ones they hope to instill in their children. Parents also determine which traits they *don't* want to see in their kids. Everyday we see admirable qualities in children like Heather

Knowlton. But sadly, we see as many children demon-strating disturbing attitudes and behaviors. These are the moral weeds unattended by parents that choke out the good, children might do."

"You're right about that Auntie Anne! We don't have to look very far to see what we don't want," Ginger said. "Unfortunately, what we don't want to see, seems to be evident to some measure in Lizzie and Carter. Just last week there was an embarrassing incident that left us feel-ing like complete failures as parents."

Auntie Anne's compassionate look gave Ginger the reassurance she needed to tell the story. "Our daughter Lizzie is twelve, and like most girls that age she spends a great deal of time worrying about how she looks and what she wears. We've tried to explain to her that some things that are considered "in" right now are just too immodest. But she wants to wear them anyway because all her friends do, including her best friend, Betsy Patterson, who lives next door.

"Well, anyway, last week Betsy stopped by on her way home from the Town Center and invited Lizzie over to see her new outfits. Meanwhile, Carter decided to stir up a little trouble for his big sister. He was sure that Lizzie wouldn't be able to resist trying on some of Betsy's new clothes, and he decided to catch her in the act. So he tiptoed onto the Patterson's porch and peered in the window of Betsy's bedroom. He was just about to head back over the fence to tell on Lizzie when she saw him and screamed. Just then Mr. Patterson came around the corner of the house. Ginger slumped in her chair, not sure what to say next.

"The first we knew of this incident was when Jim Patterson escorted Carter home," Geoff said picking up where Ginger left off. "Carter began telling us that he was looking for our cat that he thought he saw on the Patterson's porch, and that's when he just happened to see Lizzie in one of Betsy's skimpy outfits."

"It's not just our kids Geoff. The other day while at the pool, I saw so many disturbing attitudes and behaviors and nothing was done about it! Big kids were bullying little kids, taking their toys, and the parents were oblivious to what was going on."

"Or," Geoff added, "they simply didn't care."

"Anyway, I felt pretty good that at least we correct our own children when they do things that are wrong. But when this incident occurred with Carter, it was as though nothing we had done made any difference. I not only felt like a failure; I felt like a hypocrite."

Auntie Anne continued to listen to her guests as she moved toward the stove to heat water for more tea.

Then, to Geoff and Ginger's surprise, she appeared to have changed the subject when she asked, "Shall we play a game of Scrabble?"

"Scrabble?" Geoff muttered as he glanced over at Ginger. Ginger nodded, not knowing what else to do or say. Playing a word game didn't seem fitting for the moment but, after all, that is why they came to visit. Wasn't it? "Sure, we can play a game of Scrabble."

"Great!" Auntie Anne said a bit too enthusiastically for Ginger. "Geoff, would you please get the game? It's there behind you, in the old Hoosier cabinet."

Geoff retrieved the box and held it for a moment. It showed years of use. "According to this box, it looks like you play a lot of Scrabble Auntie Anne."

"Oh yes, I do. When my niece and nephew are

home, we play almost every night. My nephew is very good but that's because he learned all my tricks. Now he uses them on me."

Ginger relaxing a bit, smiled at Auntie Anne's humor. Geoff placed the box on the table and in a few moments the trays were out and the three were removing tiles from the blue velvet bag. The board waited for the first play.

"Ginger, why don't you go first?" Ginger accepted the invitation and the game was underway. Ginger placed *self* on the board. Geoff followed by playing the word *true*. Auntie Anne's glanced at the board and then down to her tiles.

"Auntie Anne, what made Heather Knowlton do the right thing?" Geoff asked. "Did her parents really have that much to do with it?"

Auntie Anne looked up. "I think they did Geoff. They had much to do with it. But they started with moral baby steps." Carefully, she played the word, *tender* and continued to speak. Are you familiar with the phrase 'Minding your Northern Manners'?"

Geoff looked over to Ginger slightly bewildered.

"Northern manners, Auntie Anne?" Ginger asked. "I'm not sure that I am familiar with that phrase."

"Well, have you noticed how many of the single houses down in Charleston's historical district were built with their piazzas facing south?"

"I hadn't really noticed that," Geoff said, "but now that you mention it, I guess they do."

"That's because the family piazza was considered as much of a private room as those on the inside of the house. From an early age children were trained never to look out the windows on the north side of the house, because if they did, they would be looking right at the neighbor's south facing piazza. Such visual intrusion was considered exceptionally rude, as their little eyes would be intruding in the neighbor's private affairs. Children who learned to respect their neighbor's privacy were said to be "minding their northern manners.""

"That's really interesting." Ginger said. "When you started, I thought you were talking about people up north teaching their children about manners or something. But now that you describe it, I do remember reading about that." Ginger turned to Geoff. "You know my dear, if we could take one of those carriage rides downtown I bet we'd learn some very interesting facts about Charleston."

Geoff just smiled at Ginger hoping her suggestion would die a natural death. Right now, he wanted to know the connection between manners and morals. "If only manners were our biggest problem Auntie Anne."

"Manners Geoff, are the first step to moral courage. Heather Knowlton didn't reach her level of moral maturity overnight. She started with small baby steps, well planned by her parents."

"Small steps, like manners?" Ginger asked, now more aware of Auntie Anne's point.

"That is it exactly Ginger. Good manners lead to good morals. It's a starting point because of what they represent."

"And what do they represent?" Geoff asked.

"Manners and morality reflect our hearts," Auntie Anne was quick to respond. "Through simple gestures of kindness and concern, self-restraint and moral courage, we show the world what we believe about other people and in so doing, we invite them to evaluate our own character."

Ginger studied her tray of letters and shuffled a few tiles. "Our kids know how to say 'please' and 'thank you' Auntie Anne. And we've taught them good table manners and how to do all the little things required in the genteel Southern way." Ginger paused only long enough to placed the word *others* on the board, intersecting *tender*. The game progressed slowly.

"Auntie Anne, we live in a society where there's no agreement about right and wrong," Geoff said. "How can parents like ourselves know if we're pushing our children too much or requiring too little of them? Is there any way we can establish a moral code that all of us can agree on? I mean like the whole world."

"That's not an easy question Geoff." Searching for the right words, Auntie Anne munched on the nuts that had fallen out of her muffin. She looked up. "Do you know what *reciprocity* means?"

Geoff gave her a questioning look. "Doesn't it mean to exchange something for equal value, or something like that?"

"Yes, that's it. *Reciprocity* is an interesting word that communicates a powerful moral message. A student of Confucius once asked the great master if there was one word upon which the whole of life could proceed. Confucius replied, 'Is not reciprocity such a word? What you do not yourself desire, do not put before others.'"

"That sounds like the Golden Rule," Ginger said. "You know, do to others what you would have them do to you."

"Yes Ginger. The Golden Rule states the principle in the positive while Confucius stated it in the negative. Basically they both mean the same thing. If you want people to treat you with honesty, kindness, gentleness, respect, honor, compassion, mercy, and justice, that's the way you need to treat others. Treat other people the way you want to be treated. If you want others to return your lost money bag, you must acquire the moral courage to do the same."

"Heather Knowlton," Geoff said quietly to himself. He contemplated Auntie Anne's insights into moral philosophy and realized that she possessed wisdom that had accumulated from years of thought. Geoff felt a tinge of shame. His expectation of Auntie Anne at ninety years of age, was far less than what this woman demonstrated thus far. And now he was discovering her capacity to understand and speak to relevant social issues far exceeded his own.

"Auntie Anne, I know we came over today to play a game of Scrabble and I certainly should be paying closer attention to my letter tray, especially now that it's my turn. But, I'm losing anyway, and this conversation is very interesting to me… to us." Geoff corrected as he saw Ginger's head bob up and down in agreement. "Can we pursue this matter a little further? Because, well… I'm curious. I mean everyone knows the Golden Rule. I've just figured that not everyone practices it because everyone is different."

"You mean like Lizzie is so very different than Carter?" Ginger asked for clarification.

Geoff nodded. "If all kids are born different, can we really expect the same thing from each of them? We can read about all the Heather Knoltons of the world, but isn't she like a moral oddity? A good oddity, of course. But not everyone can acquire the moral qualities of Heather Knolton. Or, can they?"

Auntie Anne sensed that Geoff and Ginger felt both needy and curious. That meant they were ready to hear what she had to say. She studied her tray of letters and shuffled a few tiles.

Out on the water, boats moored to colorful buoys swayed from the wakes of other boats navigating up and down the river. "Geoff, do you see all those boats on the river?"

"Yes, I do."

"You won't find any two that are exactly alike," she said. "Yet, whether they're big or small, fast or slow, all of them must follow the same rules on the water. You have to guide a boat according to the navigational standards that are fair and safe for all. It doesn't matter who you are; a big guy or a little person, rich or poor. Just because boats are different, doesn't mean the standard changes. You don't change the standard to accommodate the boat."

"What you're saying then, Auntie Anne, is boaters are to mutually submit to a common standard for the welfare of all."

"You've got the point Geoff. Now transfer the same principle to children." Auntie Anne turned her attention slightly to Ginger. "Miss Ginger you said that Lizzie and Carter are very different from each other."

"Oh, they are, Auntie Anne! I noticed the difference as soon as Carter was born. Those two children are as opposite as they could possibly be."

Auntie Anne continued her line of questions with the skill of a veteran teacher. "And where are they today?"

"With their three cousins over on Sullivan's Island."

"That's five children, and I bet they are *all* different

in temperament and personality."

"Why, yes, now that you mention it. They are."

"Then based on their God-given uniqueness, which one of the five children is exempt from being honest?"

Ginger looked over at Geoff who raised his eyebrows and answered the question for her. "Well, none of them Auntie Anne."

"Which one is exempt from being kind or playing fair because he or she is different?"

"Not a one," Geoff said again. He looked over to Ginger and back to Auntie Anne. "Your point is well made Auntie Anne."

"And that point is what Geoff?" Ginger asked Auntie Anne's star student.

"It's like those boats Ginger. Some things about them are different and some things are the same. Their sizes and shapes and colors give them their uniqueness. Those are the *variables* of construction. But their ability to navigate properly and follow the rules for the welfare of all, represents the fundamentals of boating ability. That is the *constant*… right Auntie Anne?"

"You've learned this first lesson well Geoff. The uniqueness of each child has little to do with the standard of training, and a child's uniqueness doesn't limit his capacity to achieve all the social graces necessary for life. For the good of all, every child has to learn the basics of kindness, patience, humility, self-control, endurance, respect, honesty, obedience, and thankfulness. Did I leave out any?"

Wide-eyed, Geoff and Ginger shook their heads in a synchronized motion. How could they argue with that? Weren't these traits something every parent would want to see in their children? As for leaving out any, they didn't know. The fact was that several of the virtues she mentioned had never crossed their minds.

"When it comes to children, temperament and personality are the *variables* of training," Auntie Anne continued, "but virtues are the *constants*. Think of your own two children. Each one has a unique combination of aptitudes, learning style, and temperament. That's undeniable. But character training doesn't depend on these things. When it comes to molding character, how each child learns will vary, but what each one learns must remain the same. Children vary, but virtues don't. You can't be partly honest, partly kind, partly courteous, or partly respectful. You either are or you're not."

Geoff and Ginger simultaneously let out a sigh and took a deep breath. "We have work to do Ginger."

Auntie Anne looked under the table. "Missy, where's your ball? Get your ball." Missy, who'd been hovering at Auntie Anne's feet panting for attention, scampered into the other room. Soon they heard the *click, click, click* of her nails on the hardwood floor as she returned to the kitchen. With one well-aimed tilt of her nose, Missy rolled the ball to Auntie Anne. The Scrabble game came to halt as Auntie Anne took a few moments to play toss and fetch with Missy. Both seemed lost in a world of their own.

Geoff placed an *o* and a *d* around the *d* in tender to spell *odd* and then sat back to watch Auntie Anne and Missy. Soaking up the peaceful ambience of Auntie Anne's kitchen, he and Ginger contemplated their first lesson in Ethics 101.

Returning her attention to her guests, Auntie Anne asked, "Well now, whose turn is it?"

"Your turn," Geoff said.

"Let's see." She looked back and forth from the board to her letters. Then she used the *i* in *selfish* to form *virtue,* earning enough points to take the lead. She reached into the bag for more letters.

"That's a great word," Ginger said.

"A *great* word," Geoff echoed. "That's why I'm stumped."

Auntie Anne looked up from her new row of tiles. "Stumped?"

"I suppose Auntie Anne, that a child with virtue wouldn't form the habit of lying. But Carter has fallen into that habit, and punishing him doesn't seem to help."

"Oh no, punishment only keeps a lid on wayward behavior. It doesn't teach the way of virtue."

Silence filled the room. This was a new teaching for Geoff and Ginger and they understood how important it was to keep up with Auntie Anne's tutoring.

"So, you're saying that punishing Carter won't teach him anything about honesty?"

"No it won't Geoff. It may slow or stop the behavior but it doesn't instill virtue. Believe me, I've seen it all. Parents are pros at paying attention to misbehavior. They spend more time and energy trying to eliminate waywardness than showing their children what good behavior looks like. A child, who knows only that good means not being bad, doesn't know what goodness is at all."

Geoff gave a few moments of thought to Auntie Anne's statement. "I think I understand what you just said, and I guess that's what Ginger and I have been doing—trying to suppress the wrong in our children but not elevating the right. I'm afraid our kids don't know what virtue looks like. They only know what we disapprove of."

"That's it Geoff!" Ginger exclaimed. "We spend our time telling our kids what *not* to do and then expect them to know all the right things *to* do. We're always trying to sweep their moral houses clean in the hope of getting rid of all the bad stuff."

"Well put Ginger," Auntie Anne said.

Geoff went with the flow. "So that's why the moral road has been so bumpy for us. By placing all our emphasis on which behaviors to avoid, and too little on which ones to pursue, we've set our kids on an unmarked road with no signs pointing to virtuous deeds. They're on the wrong road."

"Oh Geoff, the two of you are a sharp couple," Auntie Anne said with an encouraging smile. "I learned early on when working with children that if all you do is describe bad behavior, that's the only mental image the child has. I think parents would be better off to give their children a vision of what's beautiful, good, and right."

Geoff again had to pause and let his mind catch up to Auntie Anne's words. Turning to his hostess he asked, "Auntie Anne, how do you know all this stuff? I mean, will I have to wait until I'm ninety before I figure out some of these things?"

"Ninety, Geoff? I'm hoping we will figure some of

this stuff out before Lizzie turns thirteen," Ginger said hopefully. Their gaze turned to Auntie Anne.

"To answer your question Geoff," Auntie Anne started, "I read a lot. You see, before electricity, radio, and television, we only had books. Leaning to read was the primary way to gain useful knowledge about the world beyond our neighborhood. I always believed that the ability to read is one of the greatest gifts we pass on to children. I learned the love for reading in my early childhood, and I made sure all the little ones in my care learned the love of books."

"Are you still an active reader," Ginger inquired with a softness in her voice.

"Oh, I'm afraid that I have slowed down over the

last couple of years. I can only manage about fifty books a year now."

Geoff was about to say something, but his lips paused, "Fifty books a year. Is that all Auntie Anne?"

"My point Geoff is that much can be learned from the classics about life and raising children."

The conversation paused for a moment. Ginger looked at her letters while Geoff took advantage of the time to think about what Auntie Anne had just said. Finally, Ginger placed *vice* on the board.

"Ah yes," Auntie Anne said, "vice, the opposite of virtue." It reminds me of a problem my neighbors in Massachusetts had many years ago. Their eleven-year-old daughter, Kayla delighted in tormenting her sister Haley. Oh, that girl could be so unkind! When she would tell her friends secrets, she would make it a point to exclude Haley. There was a time when Kayla read her sister's diary and shared the contents with Haley's friends. Haley was in tears a good part of the time because of the way her sister treated her. Now, it wasn't that her parents didn't know what was happening or didn't care. They did and without a doubt,

•

they corrected her. But Kayla kept it up, and as she grew older…"

Before Auntie Anne could make her point, Geoff raised his hand in schoolboy fashion. "Auntie Anne, may I please finish the story?"

"Geoff, you weren't even there," Ginger protested, "How can you finish the story?"

"Because I think I know what Auntie Anne's going to say based on what she taught us already. May I try Auntie Anne?"

"Please, be my guest."

"The problem with your neighbors sounds like the same problem we're having. Kayla's parents paid more attention to correcting her unkindness than they did showing her what kindness looked like. Her parents were *reactive* when she did something wrong, but not *proactive* when it came to showing her what was right. Am I anywhere close to being correct?"

Ginger began to think through her husband's words. Auntie Anne and Geoff were making sense. She realized that she expected her children to do what was right, and when they didn't, she corrected them with punishment. Yet, she never went out of her way to encourage the good by showing them what virtue looked like and praising them for virtuous acts. How could she have missed what now seemed so obvious?

"More than close, Geoff," Auntie Anne said. You hit the bull's-eye. Without the knowledge of virtuous behavior, Kayla didn't know what kindness looked like. She never learned to treat others kindly, and therefore was not treated kindly by others. This resulted in a very unhappy young adult.

"Oh, Auntie Anne, it's that reciprocity thing, isn't it?" Ginger exclaimed!

"Yes, I'm afraid it is. Kayla reaped in her own life what she had sown in the life of her sister. That's how reciprocity works in the relationships that aren't based upon virtue. That is why it is never too early to teach your children about virtues."

"Starting with baby steps like, minding your northern manners?" Geoff said recalling Auntie Anne's first lesson.

"That's it Geoff." Meanwhile, Missy went to the back door, sat down, and looked at Auntie Anne over her shoulder to indicate that she wanted to go outside. Auntie Anne excused herself, rose from the chair, and let her out. Missy charged down the steps to the yard, as if in pursuit of an invisible intruder. Having demonstrated her canine courage, she meandered along the fence, sniffing.

"Let me show you something out here." Auntie Anne motioned for Geoff and Ginger to join her. They all welcomed the break and a chance to stretch.

Auntie Anne pointed to a humming bird feeder hanging from the bottom limb of a large magnolia tree. "No takers yet," she said. "It's good stuff, just what those little birds need, but there hasn't been one single visitor." She looked Geoff in the eye. "Why do you suppose that is?"

After spending an afternoon with Auntie Anne, Geoff knew one thing: This question wasn't about birds. "Maybe they didn't get your memo?" Geoff smirked at his clever reply. Ginger poked him in the ribs and gave Auntie Anne an apologetic look.

"Well maybe," Auntie Anne said, smiling at the two of them. "But I think it's because the feeder was empty for a long time and so the humming birds stopped coming. Even though it's been refilled, it will take them some time to discover the good nectar within."

The couple looked out at the Wando River, its surface gleaming from the afternoon sun. Only an hour of daylight remained.

"Auntie Anne," Geoff began, "I understand that my children are like the precious birds finding food. The food they should be feeding on is the sweetness of our goodness, like honesty and kindness, gentleness, dignity, and integrity."

She nodded, "It is as you say, Geoff. But they must discover those qualities in you. The moral resources necessary to teach your children the virtuous way must first be in your heart. Is your cylinder full? Because if it's not, your children will feed someplace else."

Auntie Anne paused, looked at the feeder and then back to Geoff and Ginger. "Listen kids, if the prescription for moral living is not written on the hearts of Geoff and Ginger, it will never be sufficiently passed on to your children. Be sure of this, the moral standard imposed on children must also apply to parents. A double standard is bad feed. A father cannot lecture on honesty and then, when the phone rings, say to his wife, 'Tell them I'm not home'."

Geoff flinched. "Ouch. That hurt, Auntie Anne." Looking toward the river, Geoff shook his head. Ginger put her hand on his arm.

"It's all about me," Geoff said. "All along I wanted to fix the little guy, and now I am learning that I'm the one who needs fixing."

"No Hon," Ginger said. "It's all about *us*." Today I've realized that Lizzie has trouble making wise moral choices because my parenting has been reactive. Censoring her choices in clothing isn't the same as modeling the modesty that can only come from a pure heart."

Auntie Anne returned to the table and game. Geoff and Ginger followed casually behind and sat down. The afternoon has not turned out like anything they had expected. They knew she was a good cook and a not so bad scrabble player even at ninety. But the philosophical side of Auntie Anne was more than a bonus discovery. It was life changing.

The game board looked inviting, drawing them once again into the safety of concentration. Geoff thought about the best way to use his *q,* while Ginger stared into space, thinking about how to be a better example to her children.

After a few minutes of concentration, Geoff used the available *u* in *virtue* to put *quiver* on the board.

"Nice," Ginger murmured. "What is that anyway?"

"It's the thing that holds an archer's arrows," Geoff said.

"I think it also means to tremble," Auntie Anne added.

"Auntie Anne," Geoff began slowly, "suppose I start living an exemplary moral life. No little white lies, like telling the neighbor that the power washer he saw me using belongs to my brother just because I don't want him borrowing it. Or, instead of thinking of myself, spending a Saturday helping a widow move furniture, or starting to show more consideration and kindness to strangers in need. Suppose I do these things and more. Will my son stop telling lies? Will my daughter want to dress modestly? Will our lives be full of moral bliss?"

"Aahh, how do the arrows fly from the bow to the target?" Auntie Anne rocked her body slightly as if she were sitting in her favorite chair. Missy saw the motion and came to her side, looking for an invitation. "Come on Missy," she said, tapping her lap. Missy was up in a flash.

The letters in the blue velvet bag were gone. All that remained were those on each tray. Auntie Anne searched the board thoughtfully. Then she used her last two letters, *w* and *y,* on either side of the *h* in *brother* to form the word *why.* The game was over but no one paid attention to that fact.

"Give your children the moral why," she said.

"What do you mean Auntie Anne?" Ginger asked.

"Well, Ginger, let me ask you. You said earlier that your kids know the basics of good manners. Is that right?"

"Yes, I did say that. But… well… I believe that's the case, but now I'm not so sure." Ginger sat back and sighed. "Their manners may just be an outward show that doesn't reflect what's really in their hearts."

"The difference between the head and the heart is the *why* of behavior," Auntie Anne said. "It's not enough for children to *act* morally, they need to *think* morally, and that happens when parents provide the moral *why* behind their instructions."

"That's different I gather, from sitting them down and lecturing them when they do something wrong." Geoff said dryly.

Auntie Anne nodded. "Too often parents tell their children what to do, and how to act, but they don't give the moral why behind their instructions."

Ginger jumped in on the conversation. "If I under-stand you correctly, you're saying that mechanical cour-tesies aren't good enough. It isn't enough to tell Lizzie and Carter that they should smile and say 'please' and 'thank you' and speak respectfully to others."

"You're thinking correctly Ginger. Behind every moral action there's a *'why principle'*." Auntie Anne stressed the last two words. Knowing and communi-cating the moral why is the secret of raising a self-directed moral child. Without the *why*, you just raise a moral robot programmed to respond on cue. Auntie Anne looked directly into Ginger's eyes. "For example, why do you say 'thank you' when someone compli-ments you or does something kind for you?"

Auntie Anne's question caught Ginger off guard. "Well… no one has ever asked me that before. Why *do* I say thank you?" I guess it's to acknowledge the courtesy of another. It's a way of paying tribute to their virtue."

"So not saying 'thank you' would be rude, and rude-ness is a vice," Geoff mumbled his thoughts out loud.

"Very good Geoff. Now here's one for you. After you've put your groceries in the car, why do you return your grocery cart to the courtesy racks provided?"

"That's an easy one," Geoff said. "I wouldn't want my cart to ding someone's car or take up an available parking place." His eyes glanced over at Ginger and she returned the look.

"Oh, don't get him started on the shopping cart thing, Auntie Anne. Our new van got dinged last week by two carts that people just deposited in the lot. The wind pushed both of them into our van."

For no apparent reason, other than agitation over hearing the word *dinged,* Missy propped up her front half on Auntie Anne's lap and draped her jaw on the table. Her look of sheer disappointment drew chuckles from her attentive audience.

"Missy loves anything to do with shopping carts. Watching them from the car is one of her favorite pastimes. Right, Missy?" Auntie Anne said, stroking her furry friend. "For us, the carts are something else entirely. It's the Golden Rule in reverse. Someone didn't consider how their carelessness would impact other people—like you."

"That's how it seems, Auntie Anne, which is why I always ask the kids to take the shopping cart back to the front of the store."

Auntie Anne gave Geoff a thoughtful look. "Do they take a shopping cart back just because you tell them to, or do they know the moral *why* behind their action?"

"Aahh, that's another good question. I don't think I've ever thought about it until now."

"There's a mountain of difference here," Auntie Anne continued. "If you never tell your children why taking the cart back is morally right, the issue for them isn't moral at all. It's just something Dad said to do. And if they don't consider it particularly fun, they'll probably complain about having to do it."

"Auntie Anne, have you been grocery shopping with us? You just described our children," Ginger said glancing at her husband.

"Wow! Ginger, there's something I just realized," Geoff slowly began with all joy removed from his countenance. "It's becoming clearer by the minute. I've deceived myself into thinking that we have been teaching our children moral principles, when in fact we've only been programming their responses. Our kids know all the right things to do, when we prompt them, but they don't know why it is right. Maybe that is why they also lack moral initiative."

Ginger summarized her husband description with seven words, "Moral sensibility is missing in our children."

Ginger looked at her husband and then at Auntie

Anne. "Auntie Anne, will you come live with us?"

"Better yet Ginger, how about we send the kids here?"

Auntie Anne gave a hearty chuckle. "When I lived in Boston years ago, our local school recruited grandparents to serve as teachers' aides in the kindergarten classroom. I so looked forward to spending time with those children! At the end of the school day I would always ask them what exciting new thing they learned. The kids would think real hard and begin to volunteer their answers." Auntie Anne paused and smiled. "So, Geoff and Ginger, tell me, what new things have you learned today?"

Ginger's hand moved across the table and touched Geoff's sleeve. The two looked at each other.

Geoff spoke first. "Well, Auntie Anne, this may be out of order, but I know the biggest change starts with *moi*."

Ginger nodded. "Both of us need to change the way we think about teaching our children manners and morals."

"Yeah, like making sure we get into the habit of giving them the why behind our moral instruction," Geoff said with an air of resolve. "I really like that part."

"Me too Geoff. But first in order to make that change, we have to learn the moral *whys* ourselves."

"Like this one Ginger? Why do we take our shopping carts back to the front of the store? We're going to remember that one. It's because other people are worthy of our consideration. It is a way to show our respect to them and their property."

Auntie Anne sat stroking Missy. The last lingering rays of the sun retreated over the horizon. Nothing moved outside but a gentle wisp of a breeze off the water. Already the dusk was settling over the eastern sky.

Ginger's mind drifted back over the afternoon's conversation. "That thing about elevating good behavior and not just suppressing bad behavior, that was so helpful. And I loved the boat analogy. I'll remember that one."

Auntie Anne looked puzzled.

"You know Auntie Anne, all the boats are different, but they all follow the same rules and operate by the same standards. That's how you get social harmony, because it keeps people from crashing into one another. It all makes sense."

Auntie Anne nodded her agreement.

"Ginger and I have to set the standard and live by it ourselves. We can't just hope our kids will turn out okay; we have to direct… ah… how did you say it, Auntie Anne?"

"Their hearts," she said. "Direct their hearts."

A movement drew Missy's eyes to the window. Standing on her back paws looking out, her gaze followed some neighbors strolling toward the dock.

"Oh, visitors," Auntie Anne said. "This is a nightly ritual on the Wando. Everyone is drawn to the water to see the sun's benediction on the day."

The threesome joined the visitors in watching the sun disappear in the Western sky. Taking the cue from the sun's last rays, Geoff and Ginger rose from the table. Geoff looked at the maze of crisscrossing words on the Scrabble board. "Well, I guess you won Auntie Anne. I don't need to know my score," he said almost in a whisper.

"Well Hon, we may have lost at Scrabble, but won the bigger prize; the knowledge to raise children with great reservoirs of moral courage."

Geoff nodded his agreement and started to pick up the trays when Auntie Anne stopped him. "I'll take care of the board and the tiles, Geoff. I imagine your children will be returning soon from Sullivan's Island and you need to be there to greet them."

The last white spears of the sun's rays broke over the western horizon when the three stepped onto the front piazza. A faint sea breeze that had come in with the afternoon tide subsided and herons and cranes were now flying shoreward for the approaching night.

Geoff and Ginger climbed into the golf cart. Auntie Anne stood watching them, all the while carrying on a conversation with Missy, who cocked her head and listened.

Auntie Anne saw Ginger look back, and then the Portiers disappeared from view as the cart turned the corner and putted down the street. In a shaggy willow tree, a mocking bird gave two or three loud preliminary trills before bursting into full evening song. Another beautiful day in the long life of Auntie Anne had come to an end.

Out on the shadowy grey of the water, a few navigational lights flickered, signaling a latecomer seeking the safety of Shem Creek. Inside the restaurant, the hostess was making her rounds, lighting the small rustic urn candles atop each table. The five couples at the big table by the window were deep in conversation. Not wishing to intrude, the hostess passed them by.

"You know, I watched her all the way down the street," Ginger said in a hushed tone. "She never took her eyes off of us, and when I looked back, I could see her head moving slightly, as if she was having a conversation with Missy."

Lela had curled her legs up into the corner of her booth seat and laid her head on Rick's shoulder. Bill held Elaine's hand on his lap, while Mac had his arm around Vicki, who was staring dreamily out at the moored boats. "What powerful insights!" Clarke spoke for the men in the group. "No wonder you were so adamant about what she could do for us. Giving kids the moral 'why' was a real eye opener."

"It really was," Geoff said. "What really hit home for me was the starting point—our own hearts."

"For me, it was the shopping cart thing." Bill added. "I could share a few stories where clearly I failed, but you might recognize me as one of those people whose carts hit your new car."

Everyone chuckled.

"Guys," Geoff said, "all I can say is that Auntie Anne never made me feel like a fool or a felon. She uncovered what was inside of me all along. And now, no kidding, we really do have a fabulous family. The bottom line is that Auntie Anne's teachings impacted our hearts."

Ginger put her arm around Geoff and squeezed him close. She smiled warmly at the other couples. "Now, let's make some plans for our second annual carriage ride tomorrow afternoon. You just never know where it might lead."

Bringing it Home
Questions for the Heart

1. According to Auntie Anne, what is the moral significance of *reciprocity?* What point was Auntie Anne making?

2. What does the following statement mean? "When it comes to children, temperament and personality are the *variables* of training, but virtues are the *constants*."

3. When teaching moral lessons, according to Auntie Anne, parents will often tell their children what is wrong and what not to do, and forget to talk about what is right and what they should do. What example did Auntie Anne use to demonstrate this point? What is wrong with this practice?

4. With whom does moral training begin and why?

5. Auntie Anne said, "The difference between the head and the heart is the why of behavior." What did she mean?

6. According to the story, how did Clarke fall short when teaching his kids to return their shopping carts to the front of the store?